The Interpreter

Motion Picture Story By
MARTIN STELLMAN & BRIAN WARD
Motion Picture Screenplay By
CHARLES RANDOLPH and SCOTT FRANK and STEVEN ZAILLIAN

Level 3

Retold by Karen Holmes
Series Editors: Andy Hopkins and Jocelyn Potter

Contents

Pearson Education Limited
Edinburgh Gate, Harlow,
Essex CM20 2JE, England
and Associated Companies throughout the world.

ISBN-13: 978-1-4058-0643-5
ISBN-10: 1-4058-0643-5

This edition first published by Penguin Books 2006
Second impression 2006

5 7 9 10 8 6 4

Typeset by Graphicraft Limited, Hong Kong
Set in 11/14pt Bembo
Printed in China
SWTC/04

Produced for the Publishers by
Graphicraft Productions Limited, Dartford, UK

Published by Pearson Education Limited in association with
Penguin Books Ltd, both companies being subsidiaries of Pearson Plc

Acknowledgements
Every effort has been made to trace the copyright holders and we apologise in advance for any
unintentional omissions. We would be pleased to insert the appropriate acknowledgement in any
subsequent edition of this publication.

© Reuters/Corbis: pg vi

For a complete list of titles available in the Penguin Readers series, please write to your local
Pearson Education office or to: Penguin Readers Marketing Department,
Pearson Education, Edinburgh Gate, Harlow, Essex CM20 2JE.

Introduction

Silvia remembered the words from the night before: "The Teacher will never leave this room." Edmond Zuwanie was "the Teacher." Did somebody want to kill him in the U.N. building? She had to tell someone.

Silvia Broome is an interpreter at the United Nations. One night she hears a plan to kill Dr. Zuwanie, the President of the African state of Matobo. Soon it is the job of Agent Tobin Keller of the U.S. Secret Service to stop the killers. He is not sure about Silvia. He knows that she is hiding something from him. What is the truth about her life in Africa? Is she telling the truth about the killers? Or is *she* more dangerous than the President's other enemies?

The Interpreter is an exciting film by Sidney Pollack, starring Nicole Kidman as Silvia Broome and Sean Penn as Tobin Keller. Pollack has made many famous movies: *Tootsie, Out of Africa*, and *Eyes Wide Shut* are three examples of his work. He is the first person to make a film inside the United Nations building in New York City.

Fifty-one countries formed the United Nations (the U.N.) in 1945, and there are now 191 countries in the organization. The U.N. wants everybody in the world to live safely, in peace. It tries to find answers to world problems and to stop wars. Its soldiers are sent to troubled areas around the world. Different parts of the U.N. do different kinds of work. The World Health Organization (WHO), for example, tries to solve health problems in poor countries.

The International Criminal Court (ICC) in The Hague, in the Netherlands, was formed by the United Nations to punish people for very serious crimes. It can also take action against heads of state who do not follow international law.

Inside the United Nations building in New York

Chapter 1   The Voice in the Dark

Matobo, Africa

The hot sun burned down on the small town. An old wooden sign above the road was shaking in the strong wind. The words on it were unclear now, but it read: WELCOME PRESIDENT EDMOND ZUWANIE.

The car moved slowly down the road. The driver was a black African man. Next to him, a fair-haired white man was writing a list of names in a blue notebook. Another white man with long, dark hair sat in the back seat, holding two cameras.

"She refused to tell me her husband's name," the white man in the front seat shouted above the noise of the wind.

"The names of the dead are bad luck," the driver replied.

"Zuwanie murdered half the town. Can their luck get worse?"

The driver slowed the car. "He can murder the other half."

The fair-haired white man put a gun and a new notebook into his bag. He and the driver climbed out of the car.

"Stay here," the driver said to the cameraman.

Slowly, the two men walked across the street toward a large, old stadium. Outside, two boys kicked a ball around the dry, brown grass.

One of the boys shouted to the two men.

"They want to show us the bodies," the driver said.

The boys took the men into a room inside the stadium. There was a strong smell of death. The men covered their noses and told the boys to go outside. In the dark corners of the room, they could see piles of bodies on the floor. "XOLA NOW!" was written in blood on the walls.

They started to check the bodies. They recognized some of the dead and found the names of others from the papers in their pockets. The white man pulled the notebook out of his bag and started to write.

Suddenly, there was a shout from one of the boys outside.

"Somebody's coming!" the white man said.

The two men ran out into the bright sunlight. There was nobody outside—only the two boys. Slowly, one boy lifted a gun and shot the black African in the chest. Then he turned to the white man and shot him in the stomach.

The white man fell to his knees.

"It's OK," he said quietly. "It's OK."

It was the last thing that he ever said.

The boy stood over the body.

"The Teacher says, 'Good day to you,'" he whispered.

Hiding in the back of the car, the cameraman took some photos. Then he quietly climbed out of the car and disappeared into the trees.

A few minutes later, another vehicle arrived. The door opened and three soldiers climbed out. A tall, well-dressed African man followed them and walked slowly toward the stadium.

The United Nations Building, New York

The main hall was full of people. Ambassadors from around the world and their assistants were listening to the Spanish Ambassador's speech. The interpreters sat in glass booths above them, repeating his words into Chinese, Russian, French, Arabic . . .

Outside the hall, U.N. Security Chief Lee Wu spoke to Assistant Chief Rory Robb: "There's a security problem at the main entrance. Put the Secretary-General[1] in the saferoom. Take the Spanish Ambassador out of the building, then get everybody out."

[1] The Secretary-General: the head of the United Nations

A U.N. guard came into the English interpreters' booth as Silvia Broome finished interpreting the Spanish Ambassador's words into English.

"Can you leave the building quickly, please?" the guard said.

Silvia, a tall woman of about thirty, with long fair hair and clear blue eyes, picked up her coat but left her music case in the booth.

"I'm teaching a student tonight," she said. "This bag's heavy and I don't want to take it downstairs. I'll get it later."

The U.N. security officers worked quickly and emptied the building. Then they took the Spanish Ambassador outside to his car.

Rory Robb watched the large black car drive through the U.N. gates. He used his radio to call his chief.

"The Spanish Ambassador has left the U.N.," he said. "He's in the U.S. again."

Silvia spent the next few hours in a restaurant with a group of other interpreters. It was nine o'clock at night when she returned to the U.N. building. She didn't see anyone as she ran upstairs.

She opened the door to the interpreters' booth and picked up her music case. Suddenly, she heard a man's voice.

"The Teacher will never leave this room," he whispered. He was speaking in Ku, the language of Matobo.

Silvia turned on a light and looked at her desk. One of the microphones in the hall below was still switched on. As the booth lit up, the man stopped talking. Quickly, Silvia switched off the light, but it was too late. She couldn't see him, but he could see her.

She was shaking as she left the booth and ran down the stairs. She heard footsteps, then a door opened and closed. Someone was following her. She ran into the nearest room—the men's restroom—and hid behind the door. The footsteps came nearer and stopped outside. Silvia pressed her back against the wall. Then, slowly, the footsteps moved away.

At the same time, on the other side of town, Secret Service Agent Tobin Keller, a tall, thin man with tired, sad brown eyes, was sitting alone in a bar. He sat there for a long time, then he went to the pay phone in the corner of the room and called his apartment.

A woman's voice on the answering machine said, "You've reached the Kellers. We're out having a good time. Please leave a message." It was his wife's voice.

He put more money into the pay phone and called the number again. And again. And again.

Chapter 2   Truth or Lies?

The next morning, Silvia went to a garage near her apartment and unlocked her motorcycle. She didn't see the well-dressed African man who was watching from his car.

Silvia moved quickly through the busy traffic. Looking in her mirror, she saw the large black car behind her. When she moved faster, the car moved faster, too. Soon it was very close to her.

Suddenly, the stoplight in front of her turned red. She rode through the light, but the car had to stop.

When she arrived at the U.N. building, she went to the interpreters' restroom. She put her purse and coat in her locker. The cleaner smiled at her and said something in Portuguese. Silvia smiled back at him, then ran upstairs to her booth.

In a room near the main hall, the French Ambassador was speaking to fifteen other ambassadors and the Secretary-General.

"There are two rebel chiefs," he said. "Xola is hiding in Africa. Kuman-Kuman is here in New York. They can't stop Zuwanie from killing people in Matobo. The killing isn't going to stop.

So we want the U.N. to send Dr. Zuwanie to the International Criminal Court immediately."

The American Ambassador looked worried. She turned to her assistant. "Get the interpreter," she whispered.

The assistant found Silvia. "We need you for a few minutes," he said, and Silvia followed him downstairs. "This is a private meeting. "We'd like you to interpret for both sides."

"What language?" Silvia asked.

"It's a meeting with the Matoban Ambassador. He'll speak Ku."

Silvia was surprised. She spoke the Matoban language, but she wasn't the U.N. interpreter for Ku.

"What's happening?" she asked.

The assistant spoke quietly. "The French want to send Zuwanie to the ICC for his crimes against his people."

The Matoban Ambassador walked into the room with three other men. "This is my assistant, Marcus Matu," he said in Ku, pointing to a tall, very thin man.

"President Zuwanie is a problem," the American Ambassador said in English. Silvia interpreted her words into Ku.

"Dr. Zuwanie is our teacher," the Matoban Ambassador replied in Ku. "The rebels—Kuman-Kuman and Ajene Xola— and their friends are the problem."

"The United States doesn't recognize the ICC," the American Ambassador said angrily. "But we want President Zuwanie to leave Matobo. He can take a long vacation or spend time with his family. If he leaves, the French plan will fail. Tell him that."

"*You* can tell him," the Matoban Ambassador said in perfect English. "President Zuwanie will talk to the United Nations next Friday. He will promise to make changes to his government. The U.N. will not vote, and your problem will disappear."

He and his men walked out of the room.

Silvia remembered the words from the night before: "The Teacher will never leave this room." Edmond Zuwanie was "the

Teacher." Did somebody want to kill him in the U.N. building? She had to tell someone.

Later that day, Silvia sat in the U.N. Security Office with Chief Wu and Rory Robb.

"Why didn't you call us last night?" Rory said.

"I was scared, so I went home," Silvia replied.

"Did you see anyone?" Rory asked.

"No," she answered, "but they saw me. I didn't understand the words, but today the Matoban Ambassador called President Zuwanie 'the Teacher.' Zuwanie's coming here on Friday."

"Call the Secret Service," Chief Wu said.

Secret Service Agent Dot Woods took the phone call. An hour later, she and Tobin Keller drove across New York to the U.N. building. Tobin's bag was on the back seat of the car.

"Did you go home last night?" Dot asked. Tobin shook his head but didn't speak. "I went to a party," Dot said. "It was somebody's birthday and I had to sing. You know I can't—"

Tobin held up his hand. "Dot," he said quietly. "Stop. You don't have to talk."

"OK."

There were ten or twelve protesters outside the U.N. One man held a sign: "ZUWANIE MUST NOT SPEAK!"

At the door to the building, a U.N. policeman stopped Dot and Tobin. Dot gave him her gun and showed her security card.

"We're Secret Service," she said.

The policeman took the card and looked at it carefully. Then he typed their names into a computer.

"Secret Service!" Tobin said angrily. "Part of the United States government!"

Dot touched his arm. "He's new, Tobin," she said quietly.

The policeman picked up a phone. "You're not in the United States now, you're in the United Nations. Wait here. Somebody will meet you."

Rory Robb came to the security gate and took them to Chief Wu's office.

"Zuwanie arrives at 08:45 on Friday," Dot said. "We'll meet him at the airport and bring him here. He won't go shopping, and he won't visit the theater. He'll speak to the U.N., and then he'll leave. *Why* is he coming here?"

"The U.N. wants to take Mr. Zuwanie to the ICC," Chief Wu replied. "He's going to promise changes so they change their minds."

"Tell me about the interpreter," Tobin said, looking at a photo of Silvia.

"She was born in the United States," Wu explained. "She spent most of her life in Africa and Europe. She studied in South Africa, France, and Spain. She has a British mother and a white African father. She's worked in the U.N. for five years."

Tobin and Dot went down to the U.N. entrance hall. Silvia was talking to another interpreter, and Tobin recognized her face from the photo.

He gave her his card. "Ms. Woods and I are with the Secret Service," he said. "We protect heads of state at the U.N."

"I don't recognize you," Silvia said.

"Our faces are easy to forget. That's why we're good at our jobs."

Silvia smiled and pointed at Dot. "Is she guarding you?" she asked.

"Yes, ma'am," Tobin replied.

"I'm not a head of state," she said.

"I know," he said. "What did you hear? If you hear the voice again, will you recognize it?"

"I don't know. It was a whisper. Whispers change voices."

"Do they?" Tobin asked.

"You study faces, I study voices."

"You were in the interpreters' booth at night. Why?" Tobin asked.

"There was a security problem and I left the building," Silvia replied. "I went back later for my music bag."

"And you heard two guys," Tobin said slowly. "They were planning to kill somebody, and they were talking in Ku. Not many people speak Ku. You do."

"You think I'm lying!" Silvia protested angrily.

"People lie all the time."

"I don't," she said.

"What do you think about Zuwanie?" Tobin asked.

"I don't like him."

"Do you want him to die?"

"I want him to leave Matobo," Silvia said quickly. "That's different. I told the U.N. security officers so you can protect him. I'm not here to watch people die."

" 'Here'?" Tobin asked.

"In the U.N. I believe in this place, not in guns and war. Listen—they saw me and I'm scared!"

"You don't look scared," Tobin said.

"You don't know me," Silvia said. "You don't know what I feel. People don't always cry when they feel sad. I'll find another person to protect me."

"I'm not your protector, ma'am," Tobin said quietly. "I protect heads of state. I'm here to *question* you."

Silvia gave Tobin his card and walked angrily away.

"What do you think?" Dot asked.

"She's lying."

Chapter 3   Zuwanie and the Rebels

Tobin and Dot returned to the Secret Service offices in another part of New York. As they walked through the building, some people said quietly, "Hi, Keller." Some looked away from him.

Two men were standing outside Tobin's office. "We're Special Agents Lewis and King," one said. "We're here to help."

Tobin's boss, Jay Pettigrew, arrived. "Are you OK?" he asked.

"Yes," Tobin said. "I feel better."

"The President called me this morning. He's worried. He doesn't want Zuwanie to die over here. Get him out of the U.N. and out of the United States. Use agents from any other organization that you want."

Tobin and Dot left the Secret Service offices and went to the CIA[2]. They talked to Agent Jon Hassrow.

"Years ago, Edmond Zuwanie was a good guy," Hassrow told them. "Matobo had a very bad government. Zuwanie freed the people and they loved him. Then he changed."

He showed them pictures of Zuwanie. In each photo, the African president held a gun. Then Hassrow showed them some pictures of dead bodies.

"Zuwanie murdered 32,000 Ku this year. Every year he kills more people. Matobo is a dangerous place—and it's getting worse."

"Who wants him to die?" Tobin asked.

"Millions of people—and these two men." Jon showed them a photo of a handsome young African man. "This is Ajene Xola. He's a doctor's son and he went to school in Paris. He was a peace protester, but now . . ."

"And that one?" Dot asked.

Jon picked up a photo of an older African man with guards around him.

"That's the man with two names," Tobin said. "I read about him in the newspapers every day."

"One name, used twice," Jon said. "Kuman-Kuman. He lives here in New York. He was Zuwanie's friend, but now they're enemies. He got too close to the President's daughter. Kuman-Kuman says

[2] The CIA: part of the U.S. government. Its agents get information about governments and people who are a danger to the U.S.

9

that Zuwanie is a madman. Both Kuman-Kuman and Xola are popular, and they both want Zuwanie to die."

"They want him to die in the United Nations," Tobin said, "in front of ambassadors from 191 countries. In front of the news cameras—in front of the world." He gave Jon some papers. "This is the interpreter," he said. "Find out everything about her."

Dot drove Tobin to the Matoban government offices before she returned to the Secret Service building. Tobin went into the office of Nils Lud, a tall, middle-aged white man, President Zuwanie's head of security.

"Tell me about the interpreter," Lud said. He started to make coffee. "Is she lying? Is she pretty?"

Tobin gave Lud some papers. "This is the U.N.'s information about her. She has a Matoban passport."

Lud looked surprised. "Does she?"

"She was born there," Tobin said.

"Are you serious?" Lud asked.

"Yes," Tobin replied.

"Black or white?" Lud asked.

Tobin looked at the coffee pot. "No, thanks."

"Is *she* black or white?" Lud said angrily.

"White."

"We need to find out—is she lying or not?"

♦

That night, Silvia returned to her apartment. It was small and colorful, with African masks and photos on the walls.

She lifted the phone, then put it down. She took her cell phone out of her purse and opened it. Then she closed it and put it in her pocket. She ran out of the apartment to a pay phone, called a number in France, and listened to the message on the answering machine.

"This is Broullet. Leave a message."

"Philippe. It's Silvia. I must talk to you. Can you call me? No, don't call me—I'll call you later."

She left the phone booth and walked nervously down the street. There was a young black man behind her. A cell phone rang. The young man stopped and pulled his phone out of his pocket. "Hi, Mom," he said.

Dot watched from across the street, as she spoke into her phone to the young black man. "Agent Sample," she said, "you're too close."

Doug Sample laughed. "Yes, Mom, things are OK. My boss is a problem, but . . ."

Silvia smiled. He was just another worker walking home. She went back into her apartment building.

The well-dressed African man sat in his car on the other side of the street. He watched Silvia, Dot, and Doug Sample. Nobody saw him.

When she was inside her apartment, Silvia turned on the light in her living room, took some new notebooks out of a shopping bag, and put them on the table. She wrote an address on a large envelope and put the notebooks inside the envelope. Then she walked slowly to the window and looked down at the dark street.

On the other side of the city, Tobin was opening his apartment door. He went into the living room and looked at the photos on the wall. He and his wife were eating, sailing, laughing. There was a big picture of his wife dancing. He sat next to the phone, turned on the answering machine, and listened to a message from his wife. He listened to the same message every night.

"Hi," her voice said. "I'm sitting here, thinking . . . I made a mistake. Are you there? I want to come back. I told him. He'll take me to the airport. Will you meet me? I'll call you when I get there. I hope you haven't changed the locks."

Then there was another message, a male voice this time. "This is Officer Luper, New Mexico State Police. I want to speak to Tobin Keller. Please call me at 812-HIGHWAY. Thank you."

Then a third message from a different man: "This is Doctor Cleary, calling from Albuquerque General Hospital. I'm sorry, but—" And Tobin's own voice: "Yes? Hello?"

The final message was from Dot. "Tobin? Are you there?" she asked. "I just heard. I . . . I don't know what to say. I'll call you later. I'm thinking about you." And the recording ended.

Tobin looked around the empty room. Then he picked up a bag and left the apartment.

Chapter 4   The Photo

The next morning, Silvia sat in a small office in the Secret Service building.

"Put your hand in this machine," an agent said. "I'm going to ask you some questions. The machine will check your answers."

Tobin and Nils Lud watched through a one-way window.

"I have some information," Lud said. "Her parents had a farm in the Mukwa Mountains. In the 1980s, the mountains were full of rebels and soldiers. Her parents were driving her younger sister home from school, and they were killed by accident, by Dr. Zuwanie's soldiers."

"How old was Silvia?" Tobin asked.

"Twelve or thirteen," Lud replied. "She will never forget—or forgive—Dr. Zuwanie. I think she wants the U.N. to send him to the ICC."

The agent came into the room. "Can you come with me, sir?" he said to Tobin. "I've done the test, but the results aren't clear. I don't know if she's telling the truth."

They left the room. Lud watched Silvia through the window, and then he went quietly into the office and stood behind Silvia.

"How were the results?" she asked.

"I don't know," Lud replied.

Silvia turned quickly. Lud smiled and held out his hand.

"I'm Nils Lud, Dr. Zuwanie's head of security. I want to ask you some questions, too." Silvia watched him carefully as she shook his hand. "What's your opinion of Dr. Zuwanie, Ms. Broome?" Lud asked. "Do you believe that he's a good man?"

"I believe in peace and quiet, Mr. Lud," Silvia said. "That's why I'm at the U.N."

"You are not an ambassador. You only interpret." He stopped for a second, then continued. "You heard a whisper. So it will probably be difficult for you to recognize the speaker?"

Silvia looked at him. "Maybe," she said slowly.

Suddenly, Lud moved closer to her. "Tell me . . . do you have a brother?" he asked.

Silvia pulled away from him. The door opened and Tobin walked in. He looked angrily at Lud, then spoke to Silvia.

"You can go. An agent will take you back to the U.N."

Silvia left the room quickly, and Tobin turned to Lud.

"There are no results from the test," he said coldly. "But I believe her. And next time you want to question an American in the United States Secret Service offices, ask my permission."

As Silvia and Lud left the building, Tobin and Dot showed some other agents the pictures of Zuwanie, Xola, and Kuman-Kuman.

"I'm from Brooklyn," Agent Mohammad said.

"OK, Mo. You can follow Kuman-Kuman. You and—"

Another man spoke. "I was with him when he first came from Matobo."

"OK, Agent Ostroff, you can work with Mo. Now, Xola," Tobin continued. "The CIA has a list of his friends here in the U.S. We'll get it soon. We're looking at the protesters, too."

Pettigrew came into the room. "I want to talk to you and Dot," he said to Tobin. They moved away from the other agents.

"What's happening?" Pettigrew asked.

"She only heard a whisper," Tobin said. "She won't recognize the voice."

"The killers don't know that," Pettigrew said.

"Wait a minute, Jay," Tobin protested. "That puts Silvia in danger. They'll try to stop her . . ."

"We've only got three days," Pettigrew said angrily. He turned and walked away.

An hour later, Tobin had a call from Nils Lud.

"I'm sending you a photo. Can you print the front and back of it?"

"Yes," Tobin replied. He looked at his computer and waited for the picture. "Listen," he continued. "I need the names of everyone in the U.N. who arrived from Africa in the last six months, and a list of everyone at the Matoban offices here."

"Why?" Lud asked.

"We want the interpreter to listen to their voices," Tobin said.

"It was only a whisper . . ." Lud said slowly.

"She wants to try. She thinks she can recognize the voice."

Lud was silent for a minute, then he said, "Do you have the photo? Look at it carefully. It's a protest against Zuwanie. The speaker is Ajene Xola. Look at the crowd . . . look closely."

There was a young white woman in the crowd. The picture wasn't clear. Was it Silvia?

Chapter 5   The African Mask

It was early evening and there were more protesters outside the U.N. building. Tobin sat in the main hall.

"When Zuwanie speaks, this room will be full of people," he said to himself. "Will the killer be here too? How will he try to kill the President?"

Silvia came in behind him. "Do you have any more information?" she asked.

"A little," Tobin said. He took the photo out of his pocket and put it on a desk. "Is this you?"

Silvia turned over the photo. There were names on the back.

"It was a peaceful protest," she said. "I was listening."

"And after you listened?"

"You're asking the wrong questions," Silvia said angrily. "Why was this picture taken? Why were the names written on the back?"

"Because it's important information. We do the same thing here in the U.S."

"In Matobo, it's different. A protest is a crime in Matobo. And this is a death list. Who gave you this—and why?"

"You're hiding something," Tobin said. "What is it? How do you feel about Zuwanie?"

"I feel . . . sad," Silvia said slowly.

"Don't you feel angry? Don't you want Zuwanie to go to court? He hurt you, his soldiers killed your—"

She touched his mouth with her hand.

"Shh," she said. "We don't name the dead." Slowly, she took her hand away from his face. "Everyone is angry when they lose someone. But in Africa, in Matobo, it's different. To stop sadness, you must save a life. That's what the Ku believe. When someone is murdered there's an all-night party one year later, next to a river. In the morning, the dead man's relatives bring out the killer, tie him up, and put him in a boat. They take him out onto the water and throw him in. He can't swim. The family can watch him die, but they will always be sad. The act of saving him will take away their sadness. They will realize that life isn't always fair." She stopped for a few seconds, and then she said, "It's too easy to take a life." She pointed at the photo. "That was a long time ago. I'm leaving. I have a class."

Later that night, Silvia sat in her apartment and thought about Africa. She remembered the open spaces and the animals, the sound of African music, and the hills in the early morning sun. She closed her eyes. She remembered an African man, the man that she loved.

She opened her eyes and looked at her photos. Then she looked up at the African masks on the wall. One was missing!

The telephone rang and she ran to it.

"Hello?" she said nervously. "Philippe? Hello?"

Nobody replied. She put the phone down and turned to the window. A man was standing on the fire escape. He was wearing the missing mask and he had a cell phone in his hand. He put his finger to his mouth and whispered, "Shhh."

Silvia screamed.

When Tobin arrived at Silvia's apartment twenty minutes later, there were already a lot of police officers and Secret Service agents outside the building.

"What happened?" Tobin asked Dot.

"Somebody took a mask from the wall," Dot said. "He went up the fire escape. When she saw him, he put a finger to his mouth. Somebody doesn't want her to talk."

"Did Doug see him?" Tobin asked.

"No, he missed him. He feels really bad. A lady across the street called the police."

Doug came into the apartment, holding the mask. "I found this on the roof."

An agent looked closely at it. "There's a hair inside it. We'll test it. It'll help us to find him."

Tobin walked across the room to Silvia. "Who has a key to your apartment?"

"Nobody."

"And the door was locked. Where do you keep your key?"

"In my purse," Silvia said.

"Have you had your purse with you all day?" Tobin asked.

"Yes—no. It was in my locker at the U.N." She was shaking.

"So, you're sitting here having a nice quiet evening at home. Then a man in a mask waves to you from the fire escape."

"Yes." Silvia almost smiled. "That's what happened."

Tobin turned to Dot. "I want somebody to look at her locker. Look for fingerprints. I'm taking her out for an hour."

They went to a bar and sat at a back table. A waitress brought them two beers, and Tobin looked at a photo of the mask.

"Is this a special mask?" Tobin asked. "A war mask?"

"No," Silvia replied. "It's a mask of peace. It was a gift."

Tobin looked more closely at the photo. "What are those words inside it?"

"They say: 'I promise,'" Silvia said slowly. She was silent for a minute, then she continued. "I'll be honest with you. My brother gave it to me. I still have a brother, Simon, in Matobo."

"What was the promise?"

"I don't know. I didn't ask him. We . . . we haven't spoken for a long time."

"What does your brother believe in?" Tobin asked. "Does he hold a gun, or does he believe in peace too?"

Silvia thought about her brother and smiled. "He believes in lists. When we were children, we lived on a farm. We were often bored. I read—and fought with my brother. He kept lists of strange facts in cheap notebooks. He had one notebook for his favorite words. That's probably how I became interested in words."

"Is he part of all this?" Tobin asked. "Why did the killers only try to scare you tonight? Why didn't they kill you? If you can recognize the voice—"

She looked at him sadly. "You don't believe anything I say. We're standing on opposite sides of the river, aren't we?" she said.

"Give me a reason to get to the other side," Tobin said.

They finished their beers and Tobin took her back to the apartment. The agents and police officers were gone. Silvia stood at the door while Tobin checked the rooms, the closets, and the fire escape.

"OK, come in," he said. "There's a police car outside. They'll watch you until tomorrow morning."

"And then?" Silvia asked.

"I don't know. I'll think of something."

"Thank you." Her voice was very sad.

Tobin moved toward the door, then he stopped. "My wife was killed," he said. He didn't turn around or look at her. "Two weeks ago. She . . . she left me and went away with another man. She was coming back . . . She was a dancer. Eddie was a dancer, too. He was a great dancer but a bad driver. He drove into a bridge outside Santa Fe on the way to the airport." Tobin stopped, and then he said, "So I can't take her back this time."

He turned and looked at Silvia. "I'm happy that Eddie's dead. I wanted to kill him. That's not very Ku." He looked around the room. "If you need anything, go downstairs. Or call the police. Or call me." He wrote his cell phone number on a card.

Doug and Dot were waiting outside the apartment building.

"We found an empty apartment on the opposite side of the street," Dot said. "We can watch her from there."

"Mo and I will watch her tonight," Doug said. "Lewis and King are with Kuman-Kuman."

"OK," Tobin said. "I'm going home. Call me if there's a problem."

Later that night, the well-dressed African quietly opened the door of a small, dirty apartment in the Crown Heights area of New York. Another African man was sleeping on the bed. The well-dressed African shook him awake.

"Hello, Jamal. Where's the mask?" he asked.

"It fell," the other man said. He was scared. "I was running. I didn't leave any fingerprints—I was wearing gloves."

"On your *head*? Did you leave any hair in the mask?" the well-dressed African shouted angrily. He hit Jamal hard. Then he pushed his face down into the bedclothes until Jamal stopped moving.

Five minutes later, he left the apartment. He climbed into a large black car. Nils Lud and Marcus Matu were sitting in the back seat.

Chapter 6   The Search for the Cleaner

The following morning, Tobin met Rory Rudd in the U.N. building.

"The door of her locker was clean," Rory said. "There were no fingerprints on it. Somebody had a key, used it, and then cleaned the locker. We're looking for a cleaner."

"Or another interpreter," Tobin said. He called Doug.

"Go down to the interpreters' restroom and talk to the cleaner," he ordered. "Take somebody with you. Find out about that locker."

An hour later, Doug and another agent, Russell, were trying to talk to the cleaner.

"Did you clean around these lockers yesterday?" Russell asked.

The Portuguese cleaner didn't understand the question, so Russell asked him again. The cleaner shook his head.

"I wasn't working," he said slowly. "Yesterday Jamal worked for me."

Russell looked at his papers. "Jad Jamal," he said. "He lives in Crown Heights."

The two men left the U.N. Soon they were in Crown Heights, running up the stairs to Jamal's apartment. They knocked loudly on the door.

The well-dressed African opened the door and looked calmly at the two agents. He wasn't wearing a jacket and he was holding a towel in his hand.

Doug showed his security card. "Secret Service," he said. "We want to talk with Mr. Jamal."

The well-dressed African smiled and shook his head.

"He doesn't understand English," Russell said to Doug.

Doug tried again. He showed Jamal's picture to the African.

"Does this guy live here?"

"No . . . not here . . ." the African said. He opened the door. "You want to see?"

Doug gave him a card. "Tell him to call this number. Soon."

The agents ran down the stairs and out of the building. The well-dressed African smiled again, closed the apartment door, and threw the card onto the floor.

Back at the U.N. building, Silvia was upstairs in the interpreters' lunch room. She picked up a newspaper and looked at the front page. There was a story about Kuman-Kuman in New York: "Kuman-Kuman—a man of the people who now takes the bus."

Suddenly, Silvia had a plan. She threw down the newspaper and ran to the door. When she reached the doors to the U.N. building, a woman stepped out in front of her.

"Ms. Broome." Silvia turned, surprised. "I'll take you home," Dot said.

As they climbed into the back of a Secret Service car, they didn't notice a man watching them. He was unshaven, and his eyes were red with tiredness. His long, dark hair was dirty.

"Tobin is sometimes difficult," Dot said. "I'm sorry. He's having a bad time." Silvia didn't answer. She was looking out the car window. "He . . . lost his wife."

"Did you know her?" Silvia asked.

"She was a dancer."

"Are you in love with him?" Silvia asked.

Dot turned quickly and looked at Silvia. There was a long silence, then she said, "Sometimes."

The car stopped at Silvia's apartment and she got out. She smiled at Dot, then ran up the steps into the building. A few minutes later, she was sitting at her desk when the phone rang.

In the apartment across the street, Dot listened to the call with Agents Lewis and King

"Hello?" Silvia said.

"Silvia, it's me—Philippe."

They spoke quickly in French, then Silvia put down the phone. She picked up her coat and left the apartment.

"I'll follow her," King said.

Silvia ran into the street and climbed onto her motorcycle. King got into his car. There was a lot of traffic, but Silvia moved quickly through it. King couldn't follow her. He called Dot.

"I lost her," he said angrily.

He drove through the streets—and then he saw her.

Chapter 7   The Cameraman

Silvia met Philippe in a park on the east side of the city. He kissed her and they sat down on a wooden seat. She looked at his long, dirty hair and his tired eyes.

"Is Simon part of this?" Silvia asked. "Are *you* part of it? Why are you here?"

Philippe looked at her. His silence scared her.

"I've done something terrible," he said in English. "Somebody called me—one of Kuman's people. I *thought* it was one of Kuman's people. He wanted to organize a meeting with Xola.

'We have to work together,' he said. 'It's the only way we can fight Zuwanie.' "

"What happened?" Silvia asked.

He took her hands. "I told Xola. I was excited. I thought that it was the end of the fight between them. But we were tricked. Xola's dead."

Silvia tried to pull her hands away. "I knew he was dead," she whispered. "I felt it. Who was with him?"

Philippe shook his head and looked away from her, across the park.

"No, Simon wasn't there. Just Xola. I stayed in the car. Nobody came back out."

"Where's my brother?" Silvia asked.

"I don't know," Philippe said. "He's hiding somewhere. I don't think they have him."

"Have him? You think Kuman has Simon?"

"I don't know. It's all crazy. We try to stop the fighting, but we can't. People see my photos in the newspaper and turn the page. You were smart to leave the country."

"I can't forget completely," Silvia said. "Simon is still there. I have to find him. I have to know he's OK."

Philippe was almost crying now. "Do you understand what I did? I took Xola to them," he said.

"You didn't know," Silvia said.

"I have to go. I'm sorry. I tried to help . . ."

"You didn't kill Xola," Silvia shouted, as he walked away.

King watched Philippe leave the park. He followed him to the Chelsea Hotel, then he called Ostroff.

"Stay with him," he said.

As Silvia got off her motorcycle outside her apartment building, Tobin ran up to her.

"You can't disappear! You have to tell me where you're going," he said angrily. "How can I protect you?"

"That's not your job," Silvia said. "Remember?"

"It's different now, since the man in the mask," Tobin said slowly. "We're watching you from an apartment across the street. Who was the man in the park?"

"It's personal," Silvia said quickly.

"No. No, I need to know. What's his name?"

"It's not your business," Silvia said, and started to walk away.

"We have your phone records. You called someone," Tobin said. Silvia stopped. "You called him, didn't you? The night before you went to Chief Wu. Before you told us about the voice in the hall. Why? Is he part of the plan to kill Zuwanie?"

Silvia looked worried. Tobin continued.

"Was that him? Here? Now? In my country? This *is* my business."

"You're wrong," Silvia said. "It's *not* your business." Then she turned away from him and ran up to the apartment. She locked the door and walked into the living room.

There was an old wooden box on the table. She opened it and took out some photos: Silvia on the farm, age 15; Silvia and Simon in front of a fire; Silvia, Simon, and Xola in a café in Paris.

It was late, but Silvia couldn't sleep. She turned on the TV and watched the news. There were pictures of Zuwanie in Africa and of the protesters outside the U.N. building.

"Is Dr. Zuwanie in danger during his visit to New York?" the reporter asked. "As we can see, the police are closing the roads to the airport."

Kuman-Kuman was interviewed. "How is a madman able to speak at the United Nations?" he asked angrily. "He'll lie about changes that he's never going to make. Zuwanie wants to stay in Matobo as president. People only have to *think* that someone is trying to kill him. That's enough to make him stronger."

Dot sat in the apartment across the street and watched Silvia through the window. The apartment door opened, and Tobin came in. He was carrying a bag.

"She can't sleep," Dot said. "She just turned the TV on."

She picked up her purse.

"Where are you going?" Tobin asked.

"Home. You're here with your bag, so I can go now." She put her hand on his shoulder. "I'll see you in the morning."

Tobin watched the news program on TV. Suddenly, his cell phone rang.

"Keller," he said.

"I'm sorry," Silvia said. "I didn't know you were watching me earlier."

"Tell me what happened," Tobin said.

"I had to meet someone."

Tobin looked at the photos on the desk. They showed Silvia and the man in the park.

"Philippe Broullet," he said. "He takes photos for a French newspaper."

"He wanted to talk to me."

"And now you're watching TV because you can't sleep," Tobin said. "What did he say to you?"

Silvia looked at the window. "How do you know . . . ? Are you across the street?" She moved to the window and saw him.

"Philippe told me . . ." she said softly. "We lost a friend. *He* lost a friend. I lost somebody that I loved a long time ago. I spend a lot of time trying to remember Africa. Now it's everywhere." She was silent for a minute, and then she continued, "Why am I calling you? What do you do when you can't sleep?"

"I stay awake," Tobin said. He heard her laugh. "You don't name the dead," he continued. "Why? What happens?"

"You move past them," Silvia said softly. "You leave them behind. You're having a hard time . . ."

"Yes," Tobin said. "And I know you are, too."

They were both silent, then Silvia said, "Will you be there until the morning?"

"Yes, I'll be here."

"I'll try to fall asleep while we're on the phone. Is that OK?"

"That's fine," Tobin said.

He watched her through the window. She went into the bedroom and lay down. The phone was still in her hand. It was quiet for a long time, then she whispered, "Goodnight."

"Goodnight," Tobin said into the phone.

Chapter 8   The Bomb on the Bus

Next morning, Silvia left her apartment and walked down the street. King sat in his car and watched her.

"Please don't take the motorcycle," he said to himself.

She walked past the bike to King's car, opened the back door, and got in.

"You can drive me," she said calmly.

They drove silently through the New York streets toward Brooklyn. Suddenly, Silvia said, "I'll get out here."

King stopped the car. After Silvia climbed out, he called Tobin on his cell phone.

Tobin was in the Secret Service offices with Russell and Dot.

"She's where?" he said. King told him the name of the street.

"Kuman-Kuman lives near there!" Tobin said. "Stay in your car, but follow her."

He turned to Russell. "What happened?" he asked.

"Jad Jamal was working in the interpreters' locker room," Russell said, "on the day that the man in the mask climbed the fire escape."

"Bring him to me," Tobin said.

"We can't find him. He wasn't home yesterday, and he didn't come to work this morning."

"Go back to his apartment," Tobin said angrily.

"Doug's already there," Russell said. He was looking at the pictures on Tobin's desk. "Hey!" he said, suddenly excited. "This guy lives with Jamal." He picked up a picture and read the name on the back: "Jean Gamba, Gabon, Africa."

Jean Gamba was in the Crown Heights apartment. He smoothed down his sharp suit and straightened his tie. He threw some papers on the floor, picked up a big bag, and left the room.

Doug was sitting outside the apartment. He called Russell.

"Jamal's friend left the building."

Tobin took Russell's phone. "Stay with him," he said to Doug. He put down the phone and turned to Dot. "We're going to Crown Heights," he said.

Tobin and Dot drove quickly through the city. They took out their guns and went slowly into Jamal's apartment. Dot opened the kitchen door.

"In here!" she called to Tobin.

There were boxes, bottles, and a lot of black plastic on the kitchen table. The room was a bomb factory.

Dot went into the bedroom, but it was empty. Then she saw that the closet door was open. She moved closer—and found Jad Jamal's body.

"Keller!" she shouted. He didn't reply, so she went back into the kitchen.

"We have a dead body in the closet," she told him. "I'll call for help. It's very dark in here—how can you see?" She moved toward the light switch.

"Wait!" Tobin cried, his eyes on the light above them. Her hand stopped and she looked up. The light was covered with black plastic. It was another bomb! Slowly, Tobin and Dot moved out of the kitchen and down the stairs.

At the same time, Doug was following Gamba. At the subway station, both men got on a train. Gamba held his bag on his knees. When the subway train stopped, Gamba got off. Doug waited for a second and then followed. They walked up the stairs onto the Brooklyn streets. Gamba walked to the bus stop and got in line.

A few hundred meters away, Mohammad was watching Kuman-Kuman's apartment. He saw the rebel leader leave his building and walk down the street with his guards. The African said hello to a neighbor and gave some money to a homeless person. Suddenly, Mohammad saw Silvia standing at a bus stop. Why was she there? He looked down the street and saw King's car. What was happening?

Kuman-Kuman walked toward the bus stop. He and his men stopped next to Silvia. When the bus arrived, one of Kuman's men stepped in front of her.

"There's a line!" Silvia said angrily in Ku.

Kuman heard her and smiled. He followed her onto the bus. Mohammad ran to the bus and jumped on, too.

King picked up his radio and spoke urgently to Tobin.

"She just got on the bus with Kuman."

"What's she doing?" Tobin shouted.

Silvia found a seat and sat down, and Kuman sat across from her. His men looked nervously at them.

"Did you speak Ku? My language from home?"

"Yes," Silvia replied. "I'm Matoban."

He gave her the smile of a man who liked pretty women.

"Do you know who I am?" he asked.

"Yes—you're a killer. You ordered the murder of Ajene Xola," Silvia said angrily.

The other men moved closer, but Kuman held up his hand.

"Who told you this?" Kuman said.

"Where's my brother?" Silvia asked.

"Your brother?" Kuman said. "Who is your brother? I don't know who *you* are. You're very brave — or crazy."

"You wanted a meeting with Xola. Your people called Philippe Broullet. You know him."

"I don't," Kuman said. "So someone wants you to believe that I killed Xola? You are wrong. You should believe me, Miss Matoban."

"Why?" Silvia asked.

"Because I want to work with Xola. We cannot win alone, but we can win together. He has people who can fight. I have money. I wanted a meeting, but I didn't ask for one. If Xola is dead, that's bad news for everyone."

The bus slowed and stopped. Jean Gamba climbed on, found a seat behind an old lady, and sat down. He opened his bag, took out a small lunch box, and put it on the floor under his seat.

Doug sat down a few seats behind Gamba. He saw Silvia, but she didn't see him. He recognized Mohammad and turned away. Then he pulled out his phone and called Tobin.

"We have a problem," Doug said. "Gamba and I just got on the 33 bus. With Mohammad. And Silvia Broome. And Kuman-Kuman."

"You're all on the same bus?" Tobin said in surprise.

"Yes."

Suddenly, Tobin understood. The bomb factory! Gamba was on the bus with Kuman-Kuman — and he had a bomb!

"You and Mohammad, get off. And get Ms. Broome off too. Now!"

"We can't do that," Doug said. "We're moving."

"Is Gamba carrying anything?" Tobin asked.

"A bag. It's on his knee."

"Can you get to him?" Tobin asked.

"No, he'll see us," Doug said. The bus slowed down. "We're stopping."

At the back of the bus, Kuman-Kuman was still talking to Silvia.

"What do you do here—so far from home?" he asked.

"I work and I hope," Silvia replied.

"Like me," Kuman said.

"I don't think so," Silvia said angrily.

"Where do you work?"

"I'm an interpreter at the U.N."

"The U.N. is full of words. They mean nothing," Kuman said.

"You want more war?" Silvia asked.

"I want more business," Kuman said. "Countries aren't important now. Only companies, international companies."

"I think you're wrong," Silvia said.

Kuman smiled. "You're still young," he said. "What's your brother's name?"

"Simon. Simon Broome."

"You're very brave. I'll ask my people to find out about him."

"Thank you." Silvia stood up and moved toward the door of the bus. She was shaking.

King, in his car behind the bus, saw Silvia climb down the steps. He used his radio to call Dot.

Tobin was still talking on the phone to Doug.

"What's happening?" he asked.

"We stopped," Doug said quietly into his cell phone. "She's getting off. Gamba is, too . . ."

"Is he carrying the bag?" Tobin asked.

Doug couldn't answer because Gamba was looking straight at him. Then Gamba moved past Kuman-Kuman and off the bus.

"He's off the bus," Doug said. "But I think he recognized me."

Mohammad stood up and followed Gamba.

"I've got him," he said quietly, as he walked past Doug.

"Mohammad is off the bus," Doug told Tobin. "He's following Gamba and King is watching Ms. Broome. I'll stay with Kuman." Doug closed his cell phone.

"Get off the bus now!" Tobin shouted, but he was too late.

An old woman opened the bus window and shouted, "Sir! Excuse me! You forgot your lunch." She pointed at the lunch box under the seat.

Doug looked out the window and watched Gamba walk away. Suddenly, he knew . . . "Oh, no!" he thought.

There was a terrible noise, then a ball of fire. In the street, Mohammad and Silvia fell to the ground.

Chapter 9   Silvia's History

Tobin and Dot drove quickly across town to the burning bus. The air smelled of smoke and death. They saw bodies under sheets. The windows in King's car were broken and a doctor was helping him. Mohammad was sitting on the sidewalk, and Dot walked toward him. There was no sign of Doug.

Silvia and a doctor were helping a small child. His mother lay unmoving on the ground. As Silvia looked up, Tobin saw blood on her face and arms. She saw him, then turned back to the child.

An hour later, Tobin took Silvia home. For a long time she was silent, then she spoke.

"When I was a child, the driver on the school bus carried a gun. It scared me. That was sixteen thousand kilometers away. Now . . ." She shook her head.

Tobin stopped the car outside her apartment and they both got out. Silvia turned to him.

"Thanks for bringing me home," she said. She opened the door to her building.

"Why were you on the bus?" Tobin asked.

"Can we talk later?" Silvia said.

"No!" Tobin replied angrily. "I lost a man today. He was very young, only a kid. We're going to talk now."

Silvia tried to close the door, but he stopped her. He followed her up the stairs into her apartment.

"How do you know Kuman?" he asked.

"I don't," Silvia protested. "I never met him before—"

"You're lying to me again!"

"I'm not lying. I wanted him to help me."

"With what?"

Silvia shook her head. "I can't tell you. Someone will get hurt."

"Why did you leave Africa?" Tobin shouted.

"I told you—"

"Why did you come here?"

"Stop *shouting* at me!" Silvia said.

"Stop *lying* to me!" Tobin said.

"I was on a bus that was destroyed. I can't think while you're shouting!" She sat down and put her head in her hands.

Tobin took two pieces of paper from his jacket pocket and put them in front of Silvia. There was a list of names on the first piece of paper, the names of people in an African rebel group called the AFP. The second piece of paper was a photo that showed Silvia with a young white man. They were walking down a road in Africa with a number of black rebels and they were all carrying rifles. Suddenly, the room was very quiet.

"That isn't me," Silvia said slowly.

"Yes, it is."

"It isn't me now." She stopped for a minute, and then continued. "Thousands of people died in Matobo. First, we protested peacefully and then we used rifles. We wanted people to listen—just *listen*. I killed a boy. He tried to kill me, so I shot him in the head. Then I gave that rifle . . ." she pointed to the photo ". . . to my brother. 'I can't do this,' I told him. But my brother didn't listen. 'Zuwanie's still here,' he said. 'Our parents are dead and he's alive. You *can't* stop.' He never spoke to me again. I write to him but he doesn't write to me. I send him notebooks—I hope he gets them. He doesn't want to know me.

"I lied to you," Silvia continued, "because I was afraid. I don't know if my brother is part of this plan. It's possible that he's trying to kill Zuwanie. I don't know. I lied to everyone to get a job here. The U.N. can change Matobo. Words are slower and quieter than guns. But they're the only way to stop the killing."

Tobin looked at the photo of young Silvia carrying her rifle, and then he looked at the woman next to him. He went into the bathroom and found a washcloth. When he came back, he sat next to her. He carefully washed the blood from her face. She touched his hand and looked into his eyes. Slowly, she put her head on his shoulder. Tobin didn't move for a long time, then he put his arms around her. He watched her fall asleep.

In the Matoban government offices on the other side of town, Lud was watching the news on television. A reporter was talking about the bomb on the bus. There were two other men in the room: the Ambassador's assistant, Matu, and the well-dressed African, Jean Gamba.

"The interpreter was on the bus," Gamba said. "She was talking to Kuman."

"Is she—?" Lud asked.

"She got off the bus. Before the bomb."

"What were they talking about?" Lud asked.

"I don't know," Gamba replied.

"What did Kuman tell her?" Lud asked softly.

Chapter 10   Simon's Notebooks

The next morning, there were a lot more protesters outside the U.N. building. Opposite them, the Matoban Ambassador was speaking to a large crowd of reporters. Matu interpreted his words into English.

"This is why Dr. Zuwanie *must* speak," the Ambassador said. "The rebels are here in America and they want to bring fear with their bombs. This terrible attack on the bus is an attack on the U.N.!"

Silvia watched them for a few minutes and then turned away.

Inside the U.N., Tobin, Dot, Wu, and Rory were looking at pictures of Jean Gamba.

"We're searching everywhere for him," Tobin said.

"He won't get into the U.N. building," Wu said.

"Maybe he's already gone and it's finished," Rory said. But Wu and Tobin didn't believe him.

Suddenly, Dot's cell phone rang. She listened, then turned to Tobin.

Fifteen minutes later, Tobin and Dot hurried into the Chelsea Hotel and met Ostroff outside one of the rooms. Inside, a police officer was taking photos. There were cameras on the bed, and a note and a bag on the desk.

Tobin went into the bathroom where Philippe was lying in the bath. The water was cold, and red with blood.

Ostroff picked up the note on the desk and gave it to Tobin. It was addressed to Silvia. Tobin put the note in his pocket and left the hotel. He and Dot didn't speak as they drove back to the U.N.

As Silvia came down the stairs into the U.N. entrance hall, she saw Tobin near the door. He was carrying a small bag and the look on his face meant bad news.

Tobin took her outside and they sat down together.

Silvia closed her eyes. "Is it Philippe?" she whispered. Tobin was silent, and she continued. "You can tell me."

"Yes," Tobin said. "He cut his wrists. Silvia—"

"I was unkind to him," Silvia said sadly. "He was unhappy, and I shouted at him. Did he leave a note?"

"Yes," Tobin said.

"Did you read it?" Silvia asked. "Of course you did."

Tobin took the note out of his jacket pocket and handed it to her.

She shook her head. "Read it to me," she said.

"Dear Silvia," Tobin read. "I couldn't find the words, so I lied to you. Simon was at the stadium with Xola and they shot him, too. I was too scared to tell you. Simon was braver than me. You're braver than me. I'm so sorry . . . I'm so sorry."

Tobin looked up at Silvia.

"He wrote, 'I'm so sorry' twice?" she asked quietly.

"No," Tobin said. "Once. The second time was me." She smiled sadly. "I don't know what to say," Tobin continued. "My friends didn't know what to say to me after my wife's death. Now I know how they felt."

"It's OK," Silvia whispered.

"Yes," Tobin said. "I tell my friends it's OK too."

He picked up the bag and put it between them. "This was with the note." He stood up slowly and walked away.

Silvia opened the bag. There were more than thirty notebooks inside—her brother's notebooks. She opened one of them. It was full of lists, in the writing of a child—lists of sports teams, science facts, and countries.

She recognized one of the newer notebooks by its gray cover—a book that she sent him. Inside was a list of names, hundreds of names. "Ruth Vera, killed in a bus station . . . Charles Token, shot . . . Thomas Vy, knifed to death . . . Robaire Mamu, murdered in a police station . . ."

She remembered Kuman-Kuman's words: "Zuwanie wants to stay in Matobo as president. People only have to *think* that someone is trying to kill him. That's enough to make him stronger."

She remembered her parents and her sister, and the soldiers that killed them. She heard her brother's voice at the time. "Don't cry," the boy said. "I'm here. I won't leave you, I promise. I'll look after you."

She remembered her reply: "I'll look after you, too."

"Promise me," young Simon said.

She opened another of the older notebooks. There was a list of animals, and then some names: "Joel Broome, killed by Zuwanie's soldiers . . . Mary Broome, killed by Zuwanie's soldiers . . . Alexandra Broome, killed by Zuwanie's soldiers . . ." She picked up a pen and added another name to the list: "Simon Broome, shot to death."

She looked up at the sky. Her face was suddenly older and harder.

"I promise," she whispered, as she wrote another name in the notebook: "Silvia Broome, shot to death."

Chapter 11   Death of a Killer

Later that night, while Russell was playing cards in the apartment across from Silvia's home, Tobin looked at some photos. There were photos of Philippe, dead in the bathroom, and Jamal, dead in the closet. There were police photos of the African mask and the bomb-factory kitchen. He looked closely at a list of telephone numbers on the kitchen wall and copied them onto a piece of paper. He read a police report: the hair in the mask was Jamal's. There were photos of the people from the Matoban Ambassador's office. He looked at Philippe's pictures from Africa: a small town, Ajene Xola and Simon Broome walking into a stadium. The next photo showed a large black car and three soldiers. Then there was a picture of a well-dressed African man. He was climbing out of the car and walking toward the stadium. It was Gamba!

"Xola's dead . . ." Tobin said quietly.

Russell looked up from his card game. "Did you say something?" he asked.

Tobin didn't reply. He moved to the window and looked at Silvia's apartment. There was a black car outside the building and a man in Silvia's living room.

"There's somebody in there!" he shouted to Russell. He ran to the door and down into the street.

Gamba walked quietly through Silvia's apartment. The living room was empty, so he went into the bedroom. The bathroom door was closed, but he could hear the shower. He shot three times through the door, then kicked it down. The shower was empty.

Tobin ran into the room. Both men stopped, and then Tobin pointed his gun at Gamba's head.

"Drop your gun and lie face-down on the floor. Now!" he shouted.

Gamba said something in French and lifted up his gun. Tobin shot him. Then he ran into the bathroom and looked into the shower. Where was Silvia? He turned to the window; it was open and the street below was empty.

Tobin called the police and his boss, Jay Pettigrew. Russell joined them and they stood in the street outside Silvia's apartment.

"Who is she?" Pettigrew asked. "Does somebody want to kill her? Or is she the killer?"

"I don't know," Tobin said.

"Well, where *is* she?" Pettigrew asked angrily. "Maybe you can *ask* her!"

"I don't know," Tobin said again. "She's scared, but that doesn't tell us anything. Russell, check these numbers." He gave Russell the list of telephone numbers from Jamal's kitchen wall.

"What's happening, Tobin?" Pettigrew said.

"I thought that two different men—Jamal and Philippe—were the killers. But they're both dead. Somebody wants us to think it's one of them. It isn't."

"What about Silvia?" Pettigrew asked. "When something happens, she's always there. She was on the bus with Kuman—"

"I don't think she's a killer," Tobin said.

"Then who *are* we looking for?" Pettigrew said. "Zuwanie will be here tomorrow morning. We don't have much time."

A police officer brought out Gamba's body. Nils Lud arrived at the same time and looked at the dead man's face.

"Who is he?" he asked.

"Jean Gamba," Tobin said. He looked closely at Nils Lud, but Lud's face was empty. "Our bomber," Tobin continued. "I shot him."

"Where is the interpreter?" Lud asked.

"She's gone. He missed her," Tobin said.

"Can I look upstairs?" Lud asked.

Tobin sent an agent upstairs with him.

"Go home and get some sleep," Pettigrew said to Tobin.

"I'm going to wait for her," Tobin protested.

"No, you're not," Pettigrew said. "Russell and Dot can look for her. You need sleep. I want you to be awake tomorrow morning." He looked at his watch. "*This* morning. We have seven hours."

Dot drove him home. "Tobin," she said quietly, "I'm worried about you. They're not our family and they're not our friends. They're our job. *You* told *me* that."

Tobin looked out the car window. "I know," he said. "And it's true."

"She'll be OK," Dot said.

He left the car and went into his apartment. There was a message on the answering machine and he turned it on. He heard Silvia's voice, and street noises behind it.

". . . I'm fine, but I don't want to talk . . . Tobin, you were right. My brother was right. Words don't stop the killing. I've had enough . . . I'm going home."

Chapter 12   The President Arrives

On Friday morning, there were hundreds of security officers around the U.N. building. There were police officers with guns on the roof and coastguard boats on the river.

A large group of protesters stood outside the U.N. Many of them wore face masks to protect their families in Matobo.

Lewis called Tobin. "The numbers on Jamal's wall . . . There's a pizza restaurant, a store, and an international cell phone."

"Find the cell phone," Tobin ordered. "Who owns it?"

Then Mohammad called. "Silvia used a computer to get a flight. But I don't know where she's going."

"Get passenger lists for all flights to South Africa from JFK, La Guardia, and Newark airports. Find her and put her on the phone."

Lewis called him again. "The international cell phone belonged to Jean Gamba," he said.

"Did he call somebody at 3:30 PM the day before yesterday?" Tobin asked.

"Yes," Lewis replied.

"That was after the bomb on the bus," Tobin said. "Who was the first person he called? Try the number, then call me back."

A minute later, Tobin's cell phone rang again.

"It's a number in the Matoban government offices," Lewis said.

"Lud's number?" asked Tobin.

"No," Lewis replied. "Somebody named Marcus Matu. He's one of the Ambassador's assistants."

"Go there!" Tobin shouted.

His phone rang again. This time it was Mohammad.

"She's on a flight out of JFK Airport at 9:00 AM."

"Go to the airport and wait for her," Tobin said. "Then call me."

Matu and a group of Matobans arrived at the U.N. building. They walked through the security gates, past the U.N. guards, and past Tobin.

Dot was at JFK Airport when Edmond Zuwanie came down the stairs from his airplane. He looked old, small, and weak.

"Is that Zuwanie?" Dot asked the agent next to her. "Has that old man really killed thousands of people?"

Lud greeted the President. Zuwanie smiled and climbed into a car. Lud and Dot got in with him and they started to drive across the city to the U.N.

Zuwanie looked out the car window at Manhattan Island.

"I want to go to the theater," he said.

"That's not possible, sir," Dot said.

"Last time I came here, there was a lot of sky," the President said. "Now there are more tall buildings."

"You came here twenty-three years ago, Dr. Zuwanie," Lud said. "Things change."

"They get less important," Zuwanie said. "They put flowers on the bridge during my last visit. I freed Matobo and the American people welcomed me with flowers."

A few minutes later, the car arrived at the U.N. building. The protesters shouted angrily and waved their signs at the President.

He looked surprised. "Are these people here for me?" he asked Dot.

"Yes," Dot replied.

Tobin opened the car door and Zuwanie climbed out slowly. Lud took his arm and helped him into the building.

Tobin's cell phone rang again.

"I'm at the airport. I can't see her," Mohammad said.

"Stay there," Tobin said. He turned to Pettigrew. "Can we keep Zuwanie in the saferoom? It will give us more time."

"We can try," Pettigrew said. "But he wants to speak."

Tobin called Lewis and King. "Are you at the Matoban government offices?" he asked.

"Yes," Lewis replied. "But Matu isn't here. He didn't come in this morning. Nobody knows where he is."

"They know where he is," King said. "But they won't tell us."

"Get a photo of him and send it to the U.N. security officers," Tobin said. "Then go to his home address."

Two minutes later, a U.N. security officer came up behind him.

"This picture just arrived, sir," he said, and he gave Tobin a photo of Matu.

Tobin looked at it carefully—and recognized the face!

"He's here!" Tobin shouted. "I just saw him at the top of the stairs."

He left Dot with Zuwanie and ran into the main hall. It was full now with hundreds of people who were waiting for Zuwanie. Tobin saw Lud sitting with the other people from Matobo. He looked up and saw the interpreters in their booths. He looked for Matu, but he couldn't see him.

Chapter 13   Murder in the U.N.

Marcus Matu went into the men's restroom and pulled the paper-towel cover from the wall. Pieces of a rifle were hidden behind it. He put them in his bag and left the restroom, then he ran upstairs to the interpreters' booths.

One of the interpreters was sitting in a booth, testing his microphone. He didn't hear the door open behind him. Matu hit him on the back of the head, and the man fell to the floor.

Matu opened his bag and took out the pieces of the rifle. He put them together quickly and looked through the window of the booth. President Zuwanie was standing at the front of the hall.

The Secretary-General introduced him and made a short speech of welcome. Then Zuwanie started to speak.

"Mr. President, Mr. Secretary-General," Zuwanie said, "today rebels are attacking my country. They will do anything to hurt me. They even bombed a bus here in New York. How can I protect my country from enemies like this?"

Tobin stood at the back of the room, watching. Lewis called him on his radio.

"We're at Matu's address," Lewis said. "He's not here. And it's not an apartment—it's an AIDS[3] hospital. This guy has nothing to live for."

Tobin looked again around the hall and saw an empty seat. Nils Lud was missing. He looked up at the interpreters' booths. There was a small hole in one of the windows.

"Get Zuwanie out of here!" he shouted to Dot and Rory. Then he started to run.

Upstairs, Matu was on his knees on the floor of the booth. There was a hole in the glass window and he was pointing the rifle at Zuwanie.

The door opened. Matu turned quickly and pulled the rifle back from the window.

Nils Lud was standing behind him. He was wearing cotton gloves and he was holding something in his left hand.

"You did well," he said. "Your mother and sister will get the check for the money on Monday." Matu turned back to the window and pointed the rifle at Zuwanie again. Lud put his right hand inside his jacket pocket and took out a small gun. "But I don't want you to do *too* well," he said.

[3] AIDS: a very serious illness that kills many people

Matu tried to shoot—but nothing happened. There was something wrong with the rifle. He pulled it back from the window and looked at Lud. Lud smiled, then he shot Matu twice through the head. The second shot broke the window of the interpreters' booth into a million pieces.

Glass fell on to the people in the hall below. Some of them screamed and started to run for the exit doors. Dot and Rory were already pushing Zuwanie out of the hall and into the saferoom.

With his gun in his hand, Tobin ran upstairs and into the interpreters' booth. He saw the male interpreter lying on the floor and the blood on Matu's face. Then he saw Lud. Lud was holding a small gun in his right hand. Matu's rifle was on the floor near his left hand.

"I looked up and saw him," Lud said quickly. "Luckily I was able to stop him. He's from our office."

"I know who he is," Tobin said. "You can put your gun away now." Lud put his gun into his pocket.

"He almost killed Dr. Zuwanie," Lud said. "Another two or three seconds—I was almost too late."

Tobin looked at him and remembered Kuman-Kuman's words: "Zuwanie wants to stay in Matobo as president. People only have to *think* that someone is trying to kill him. That's enough to make him stronger." Suddenly, he understood. He moved toward the rifle and started to pick it up.

"Don't touch the rifle!" Lud shouted.

"Why?" asked Tobin. "Because I'm not wearing gloves? It's warm today. Why are *you* wearing gloves?"

"What? I . . . I . . ." Lud couldn't answer.

"When the rifle didn't work," Tobin said, "Matu was probably very surprised. Did you have time to put the piece back in?" He pointed the rifle and Lud jumped back. "Yes," Tobin said. "I guess you did. But you were wearing gloves, so nobody will know. Only Matu's fingerprints are on that gun."

The door opened and two U.N. security officers came in. Lud reached into his pocket for his gun, but Tobin and the officers were quicker.

Dot ran into the room.

"Nobody is going to shoot Zuwanie," Tobin told her. "It was a smart plan. People will listen to a man in danger. They'll understand *why* he has to kill." He turned to Lud. "Are you the bad guy, Lud? Or are you working for a bigger bad guy?"

He and Dot left the room.

"Are you OK?" Dot asked.

"Where's Zuwanie?" Tobin asked.

"In the saferoom. What happened in there?"

Tobin started to answer, but his cell phone rang. It was Mohammad.

"I've checked every flight and every hotel in New York. I've asked her friends. Nobody knows her very well. They don't know where she is."

"*I* know her," Tobin said slowly. "She said 'I'm going home.' "

"Where is home?" Dot asked.

"Here," Tobin said.

Chapter 14   Silvia and the President

Zuwanie was alone in the saferoom when the door opened. Silvia walked in, carrying a bag.

"Dr. Zuwanie," she said.

"Yes?" he replied and smiled at her.

"I remember your last visit to the U.N.," Silvia said.

"That was a long time ago," Zuwanie said. "You were very young. *I* was very young!"

"We watched you on TV, back home in Matobo. My family, all the families, watched you. You were like a movie star."

Zuwanie laughed. "I don't think so!"

"You *were*," Silvia said. "We were excited and very proud of you because you were speaking to the world. But that was a long time ago." Her voice grew harder.

"What is your name, child?" Zuwanie asked.

"Silvia. You killed my family."

Zuwanie suddenly looked uncomfortable. His eyes moved around the room.

"Where is everyone?"

"We're alone," Silvia said. She moved very quickly toward him and took a gun out of his pocket. "You always carry this gun. I saw it in every picture, everywhere you went. You saved our country with this gun." She held the gun in her hand, but she didn't point it at Zuwanie. "Then you used it to kill your people."

She pulled a small book out of her bag. It was Zuwanie's life story. She opened it and read: " 'You must fight for your land and country before you can understand the importance of that land and country.' Who said that?" Zuwanie looked closely at her face, but he didn't speak. "Yes, you did," Silvia said. "I was eleven years old and I loved you. You were my teacher." She turned the page and showed Zuwanie a photo of a little boy. "Look at yourself!" she said.

"The good times are past," Zuwanie said. "Finished."

"It's not finished!" Silvia shouted. "Not until you die."

"But I'm not ready to die."

Silvia pulled a notebook out of her bag. "*These* people weren't ready to die!" she screamed. "You were a good man—and now . . . You gave your people so much—and then you took it away."

She moved toward him and placed the gun against his head.

Tobin and Dot met Chief Wu, Rory, and some U.N. security guards at the saferoom door.

"Is he in there?" Tobin asked.

44

"Yes," Wu replied. "What's happening?"

"Keep everyone out," Tobin said to Dot. "Give me a few minutes."

He stood near the door and called, "Silvia! I'm coming in. It's only me. I'm coming in now."

He opened the door slowly and looked inside the room. Silvia was pointing the gun at Zuwanie's head. Tobin saw Simon's notebook on the table in front of the President.

"Close the door," Silvia said.

Tobin looked back at Dot, Rory, and Wu. "It's OK," he said to them and went inside the room.

He closed the door and turned to Silvia.

"Don't do this. We have Nils Lud and the rifle. That's all we need."

"But I have *him*," Silvia said and pointed at Zuwanie.

"Silvia," Tobin said softly, "he's finished. Lud is, too. Zuwanie will die in prison."

"Simon didn't die in prison—he was shot. I want him to die in the same way."

"He'll die in ten seconds, but you'll remember killing him for the rest of your life." He turned to Zuwanie. "Matu is dead. Your head of security has told us everything. That leaves you."

Zuwanie opened his mouth to speak, but Tobin stopped him.

"It was a good plan," he said. "You're 'almost' murdered and people understand you better. But now it's finished. You'll go to court."

Silvia pressed the gun harder against Zuwanie's head.

"No, he won't," she said.

"Silvia, listen," Tobin said. "Remember the story about the Ku? The family can watch a murderer die or they can save him. I hate the man who destroyed my life. But I don't want to kill him."

"Then you're wrong," Silvia said.

"No, I'm not," Tobin said. "I don't want to be sad for the rest of my life."

Zuwanie picked up Simon's notebook. "What's this?" he asked. They weren't listening to him and he started reading the names in the book.

"Leave this room now," Silvia ordered Tobin.

"I can't," Tobin said. "Put the gun down."

"I can't," Silvia said.

"You can."

"Just go!" she shouted.

Tobin quickly pulled out his gun and pointed it at her. Then he slowly placed it on the table.

"See? It's easy to put down a gun." She looked at him but she didn't move. "Shoot him and he'll be dead," Tobin said. "And then you'll be dead . . . and . . . I'll be dead, too."

Silvia's hand was shaking. Suddenly, she looked at Zuwanie and pointed at the book on the table.

"Read it!" she shouted.

Zuwanie put down the notebook and picked up his life story.

"Where? Which part?"

"The first page," Silvia said.

Slowly and quietly, Zuwanie started to read: "The guns around us . . ."

"Louder," Silvia said. "Like when you wrote it. When you believed in it. When it *meant* something."

Zuwanie tried again. "The guns around us make it hard to hear. But a man's voice is different from other sounds. We can hear it over all other noises. We can hear a whisper above the noise of a thousand soldiers . . ."

"When? *When*?" Silvia shouted.

". . . when it is telling the truth," Zuwanie read. He looked at the picture of himself when he was small boy. Then he picked

46

up Simon's notebook again, and his hand moved slowly across the names of the dead.

"That little boy was my country," Silvia said.

Tobin reached out his hand toward her. She looked at him for a long time, and then she looked at Zuwanie. Slowly, she gave the gun to Tobin and he put it in his pocket.

Chapter 15   The Names of the Dead

The main hall of the U.N. was full of people again. The interpreters were in their booths.

"Dr. Zuwanie, the President of Matobo, will continue his speech," the U.N. Secretary-General said.

Zuwanie and Silvia walked to the front of the silent room. Zuwanie looked at the people in front of him, then he started to speak in Ku. Silvia interpreted his words into English.

"Nukwe wa Bamcha . . . Temsha wa Bamcha . . . killed by bombs. Bukewechu we Lali . . . Alexander Mungoshi . . . shot by soldiers. Stambuli wa Tikuu . . . Ruth Kufomo . . . killed for crimes against Matobo."

Tobin stood at the back of the hall and listened.

Zuwanie continued. "Edgar Sekuu . . . Avu wa Mfusani . . ."

"Killed in their home by a bomb," Silvia interpreted.

There were microphones inside the hall, so the protesters outside the building could hear Zuwanie's words.

"He's reading a list of the names of the dead," one protester whispered. "He's saying that he murdered them."

Inside, too, people were beginning to understand.

"Zimwe wa Ngwama . . . Dukura wa Mboko . . . holding a newborn child," Zuwanie said in Ku. "I don't know its name." And then in English: "I'm sorry." He looked at Silvia.

47

He read the names for a long time. Finally he said, "Simon Broome," and Silvia repeated, in English, ". . . shot to death."

◆

Two days later, the sun was shining on New York. Tobin was outside the U.N. building, watching the river.

Silvia came out and walked over to him. "Hi," she said.

Tobin turned around. "Hi," he said. "What happened?"

"It was OK," she replied. "They told me what you said. You don't think I'm dangerous."

"Yes," Tobin said. "I lied."

They both smiled.

"Thank you," Silvia said.

"Are you at work again?" Tobin asked.

"No," Silvia said. "They didn't believe you. I'm going home."

"Home? To Africa?"

"Yes," Silvia said quietly. "I miss it. I never had the time to tell you. I miss the animals at night, the rain, the smells."

"We've got rain here, and smells," Tobin said and pointed at the river. "There's nobody there for you in Africa, is there?"

"No," she said. "But I can remember them there."

"You can remember people anywhere," Tobin said. Silvia understood that he was thinking about his wife. She touched his arm. "My job has changed," he continued. "Who am I protecting? I need to know. Maybe *I* need a change."

"Have you visited Africa?"

Tobin laughed. "I was born in New York, and I went to school on the same street. Then I came across the river to Manhattan. It's not far."

"You're a traveler," Silvia smiled. "I've known you for five or six days—it feels much longer."

"When are you leaving?" Tobin asked.

"Tomorrow," Silvia said.

"Will you be safe? Is there another Zuwanie in Matobo?"

"No. That can't happen. We won't let it."

Tobin smiled at her. "You're already there, aren't you?" he said softly. Then he pointed at the water. "Hey, look—we're on the same side of the river now."

"Will you be OK?" Silvia asked. "Will you tell me?"

She turned to leave, but he stopped her. He pulled her close and kissed her, then she moved away.

"You'll always know," Tobin said.

Silvia walked a few steps away from him and then stopped again. "What was her name? Your wife?" she asked.

"Laurie Keller," Tobin said. "Killed in a car accident in Santa Fe. Twenty-three days ago."

Silvia smiled sadly at him and said a few words in Ku.

Tobin guessed the meaning. "Rest in peace," he said.

Silvia walked away toward the U.N. gates. She didn't look at him again, but she was still smiling. Tobin looked back at the calm, wide river and across it toward Africa.

ACTIVITIES

Chapters 1–3

Before you read

1 What do you know about the United Nations (the U.N.)?
   a What does the organization do?
   b Where are its offices?
   c What is the name of the Secretary-General?
   d What is the ICC?
   e Is your country in the U.N.? If it is, when did it join?
   f Find out about these parts of the U.N.: WHO, UNESCO, IMF, and the FAO. What do they do? You can find information about the U.N. in six languages at www.un.org.

2 Look at the Word List at the back of this book.
   a Check the meaning of words that are new to you.
   b Are these words for people or places?
      agent   ambassador   booth   hall   interpreter   rebel

3 This book is about an interpreter who works at the United Nations. Two of the other important people in the story are a Secret Service agent and the president of an African country. What do you imagine this story is about? What brings these people together? Do you think it is a mystery, a murder, or a love story? Read the Introduction to the book to answer these questions.

While you read

4 Are these sentences true (T) or not true (NT)?
   a Matobo is a country in Africa.   .....
   b Three men are killed outside the stadium in Matobo.   .....
   c Edmond Zuwanie is the Secretary-General of the U.N.   .....
   d Silvia Broome is the U.S. Ambassador.   .....
   e Xola and Kuman-Kuman are friends of Zuwanie.   .....
   f Silvia goes back to the booth for her music bag.   .....
   g Silvia was born in the U.S.   .....
   h Kuman-Kuman lives in New York City.   .....
   i Philippe Broullet follows Silvia home.   .....
   j Tobin's wife is on vacation.   .....

5 Complete each sentence with the words on the right.

a	Silvia is	a government agent.
b	Tobin is	a friend of Silvia's.
c	Rory Robb is	a rebel leader in Matobo.
d	Jay Pettigrew is	Assistant Chief of U.N. security.
e	Nils Lud is	Tobin's boss.
f	Zuwanie is	a government agent.
g	Xola is	an African president.
h	Philippe Broullet is	an interpreter.
i	Dot Woods is	Zuwanie's head of security.

6 Answer these questions.

    a Silvia goes back to the interpreters' booth at night. What does she hear?

    b What does the French Ambassador want to do to President Zuwanie? Why?

    c Why is President Zuwanie coming to the U.N.?

    d Why are there protesters outside the U.N. building?

7 Talk to another student about Matobo and President Zuwanie. Discuss the country and its history. Who are the rebel leaders and what do they want?

Chapters 4–6

Before you read

8 Talk to other students about these people in the story:

    a Zuwanie: is he a good or bad president?

    b Silvia: is she lying or telling the truth?

    c Tobin: will he help Silvia or hurt her?

    d Tobin's wife: where is she and what has happened to her?

While you read

9 Circle the right word in each sentence.

    a Silvia's parents are *dead/alive*.

    b Agent Mohammad follows *Xola/Kuman-Kuman*.

    c Lud sends Tobin a *photo/letter*.

    d Silvia has African *plants/masks* in her apartment.

e There is a *hair/fingerprint* inside the mask.

f Somebody steals Silvia's *key/purse* from her locker.

g Silvia has a brother named *Simon/Philippe*.

h Jamal's apartment is in *Manhattan/Crown Heights*.

i Tobin's wife was *an actress/a dancer*.

j Silvia calls *Philippe/Xola*.

After you read

10 Who says:

    a "Tell me . . . do you have a brother?" ....

    b "I'm from Brooklyn." ....

    c "She thinks she can recognize the voice." ....

    d "You're asking the wrong questions." ....

    e "He was a great dancer but a bad driver." ....

    f "Did you leave any hair in the mask?" ....

    g "I was wearing gloves." ....

    h "Tobin is sometimes difficult." ....

    i "Yesterday Jamal worked for me." ....

    j "I lost her." ....

11 Use the words below in these sentences.

hair   photo   apartment   dancer   masks   key
fire   newspaper   farm   African

    a Silvia's parents had a .... .

    b Lud sends Tobin a ..... of a protest against Zuwanie.

    c There are African ..... on Silvia's apartment wall.

    d Silvia sees a man on the ..... escape.

    e There is a ..... inside the mask.

    f Somebody stole Silvia's ..... from her locker.

    g The agents watch Silvia from an empty ....

    h Silvia sees a story about Kuman-Kuman in a ....

    i The well-dressed ..... is at Jamal's apartment.

12 Discuss these questions.

    a What happened to Silvia's parents and Tobin's wife?

    b How have Silvia and Tobin's lives changed as a result, do you think?

13 Why are these things important in the story?

    a the photo of the peace protest   **c** gloves

    b the African mask   **d** Jamal's hair

14 Work with another student. Have this conversation.

    Student A: You are Tobin. You want to know everything about Silvia and her life. Ask her questions.

    Student B: You are Silvia. You like Tobin, but you are a very private person. Tell him only what you have to. Ask him questions about his life.

Chapters 7–9

Before you read

15 Discuss these questions.

    a Silvia speaks to Philippe on the phone. What do you think she will do next? Why?

    b Do you think Nils Lud is a good or a bad man in this story? Why?

While you read

16 Answer these questions with *yes* or *no*:

    a Did Philippe kill Xola?   .....

    b Does Silvia get on the bus with Kuman-Kuman?   .....

    c Is Jamal's body in the closet?   .....

    d Is the bomb in Gamba's bag?   .....

    e Is Mohammad killed by the bomb on the bus?   .....

After you read

17 Answer these questions.

    a Where does Silvia meet Philippe?

    b What happened to Xola?

    c What is the name of the well-dressed African?

    d What do Tobin and Dot find at the Crown Heights apartment?

18 In what order do these people get off the bus? What happens to them?

    Jean Gamba   Kuman-Kuman   Doug   Silvia   Mohammad

19 Imagine that you are Silvia. Describe your life in Matobo when you were a child. Why did you join the rebels?

Chapters 10–12

Before you read

20 Imagine that you are Tobin. Do you think Silvia is planning to kill Zuwanie? Why? How? If she isn't, who is?

While you read

21 Who:

a	interprets the Matoban Ambassador's words?	....
b	cuts his wrists?	....
c	tells Silvia that Philippe is dead?	....
d	wrote lists in notebooks?	....
e	tries to kill Silvia?	....
f	shoots Gamba?	....
g	meets Zuwanie at the airport?	....
h	owns the international cell phone?	....
i	looks for Silvia at JFK Airport?	....
j	wore the African mask and scared Silvia?	....

After you read

22 Complete these sentences.

   a Dot and Tobin go to the Chelsea Hotel because .....

   b Simon is dead, so .....

   c Tobin and Russell watch Silvia from .....

   d Tobin sees someone in Silvia's apartment, so .....

   e Gamba lifts his gun to .....

   f Pettigrew sends Tobin home because .....

   g When Tobin gets home, he .....

   h The protesters at the U.N. wear face masks to .....

   i Dot is surprised when she sees President Zuwanie, because .....

   j Mohammad goes to JFK Airport to .....

23 Have a conversation between Tobin and his boss, Jay Pettigrew.

Student A: You are Pettigrew. Ask Tobin for information about Silvia and the killer.

Student B: You are Tobin. Answer Pettigrew's questions. Tell him your thoughts about Silvia.

24 This is President Zuwanie's second visit to the U.N. Compare it with his first visit. Why is it different?

Chapters 13–15

Before you read

25 Guess what will happen.

  a Somebody dies in the U.N. building. It is:

  Lud   Marcus Matu   Dr. Zuwanie

  b At the end of the story, Zuwanie is:

  in prison   happy   dead

  c Somebody goes back to Africa. It is:

  Zuwanie   Marcus Matu   Silvia

26 What do you think Silvia will do next? How will the story end?

While you read

27 Circle the right answer.

  a Where does Matu go for the gun?

  home   the restroom   the saferoom

  b What does Matu take into the interpreters' booth?

  a bag   a book   gloves

  c Where do Dot and Rory take Zuwanie?

  to the restroom   to the saferoom   to the interpreters' booth

  d What is Lud wearing when he goes into the interpreters' booth?

  a mask   a hat   gloves

  e What does Silvia take into the saferoom?

  a gun   a book   a mask

  f Where does Tobin say goodbye to Silvia?

  in the saferoom   near the river   in her apartment

  g Where is Silvia going?

  back to her apartment   to Crown Heights   to Africa

After you read

28 Put these actions in the correct order, 1–5.

    a Lud goes to the interpreters' booth.

    b Matu goes to the restroom.

    c Tobin goes to the interpreters' booth.

    d Matu gets the rifle.

    e Matu goes to the interpreters' booth.

29 Discuss:

    a why Silvia makes Zuwanie read part of his life story.

    b why Zuwanie reads the names of the dead.

    c what Tobin means when he says, "We're on the same side of the river now."

Writing

30 Imagine that you are a protester. You don't want President Zuwanie to visit the U.N. Write a letter to a newspaper and give your reasons.

31 Imagine that you are the cameraman Philippe Broullet before he dies. Write a report for your newspaper about the stadium in Matobo. Describe what happened to your friends.

32 Find out more about the United Nations and write about it. Describe:

    ● when it started

    ● who can join

    ● what the U.N. does

    ● where it meets.

33 You are a Secret Service agent. Tobin Keller wants to know everything about Silvia Broome. Write a report for him. Tell him about her life in Africa, her family, and her job at the U.N.

34 Imagine that you are Dot. Write a letter to a friend about Tobin and his wife's death. Describe your feelings for him.

35 Simon Broome writes lists of interesting facts. Write a one-page list of interesting facts about your country.

36 You are a television reporter. Write a report for your news program. Describe President Zuwanie's speech and the shooting at the U.N.

37 Write a different ending to the story. Who was killed? Why? What happened next?

38 Write a telephone conversation between Silvia and Tobin a year after Silvia's return to Africa.

39 Did you enjoy this book? Why (not)? What is the story? Describe it for your friends.

WORD LIST

agent (n) somebody who works for a government, often in secret activities

ambassador (n) somebody who acts for his or her government in a foreign country

bomb (n/v) something that can kill many people

booth (n) a small room inside a larger room

cell phone (n) a phone that you carry in your pocket

fingerprint (n) the lines in the skin on the end of your finger

glove (n) a piece of clothing worn on your hand

hall (n) a large room

interpret (v) to explain something in a different language

locker (n) a small cupboard with a lock

mask (n) something that covers your face

peace (n) a time when there is no war

protest (n/v) a group of angry people showing their feelings

rebel (n) somebody who fights against the government

recognize (v) to see a face that you have seen before; to hear a sound that you have heard before; to accept that an organization is lawful

rifle (n) a long gun that you hold against your shoulder

security (n) protection from danger or crime

stadium (n) a large area for sports with seats and a building around it

truth (n) the true facts about something

whisper (v) to say something very quietly